With Me

A POETIC EXPRESSION OF GOD'S FAITHFULNESS

CAROLYN STAFFIERI

FOREWORD BY LISA LYNN ERICSON

Library of Congress Control Number: 2025905410

Paperback ISBN-13: 978-1-966283-49-2
Hardback ISBN-13: 978-1-966283-50-8

Cover Image by Irina Bort / Adobe Stock
Cover Design by Marty Shaughnessy / Deklanmedia
Interior Design by Niddy Griddy Design, Inc.

To my husband John, who is my inspiration and love.

Thank you for encouraging me to step out in faith and share our story. I could not do life without you. I love sharing our laughter despite tearful times.

To our children Abigail and Nathan, none of this would be possible without you. You have walked this journey with us, you are the answers to our prayers.

To my mother, Penny. You are the greatest example of love to a daughter. Thank you for all of the selfless things you do for me.

Lisa, had you not shared your gift, none of this would be possible. You believed in me and I am beyond grateful.

And to my faithful prayer warrior, Beautiful You, your prayers have helped bring this collection to completion.

Table of Contents

Foreword

The beautiful smile on Carolyn Staffieri's face emanates from a heart that knows solid peace, a spirit that resists succumbing to earthquakes and aftershocks. Hers is not an easy smile, but for that very reason, it speaks volumes, her eyes reflecting a joy that is both calm and eager.

When she picks up her pencil, Carolyn expresses in vivid poetry the literal up and down, back and forth of her existence. Her strong conviction that God is her firm foundation cries out in sharp contrast to a life rattled by deeply relatable struggles. This is a woman who dares to claim that she is not alone, even when uncertainty or conflict could incite a dramatic collapse. Instead, she rises above life's challenges, telling through her poetic story the truth that God is alongside her in each episode.

The lines on these pages trace a captivating equilibrium between lightheartedness and earnest devotion. Most importantly, they depict the reality that God is with us, active and worthy of full trust. And so, through the power of her poetic pencil, Carolyn has transformed *with me* into *with us*, a word picture that brings a true smile to anyone's face.

Lisa Lynn Ericson
Theatre & Film Professional, Poet & Author
November 2023

Acknowledgements

Thank you to my daughter, Abigail Barstow, for her creative skills in editing photos and social media management (@allthehappycreativeco). You are beautiful, talented, and I am thankful.

Thank you, Keziah Loht, (@keziah.renee) for the photos.

A special thank you to Marty Shaughnessy at Deklanmedia for his cover design.

Introduction

Have you ever found your world upended without an explanation or found yourself asking "why" in the midst of an unfair situation?

You are not alone!

My life's journey has been unexpected and faith-tested many times, but none more than through the 30 years marked by epilepsy. Purple, the color you will find woven throughout many poems, is associated worldwide with epilepsy. I encourage you to allow purple to wash over your own scars as you read, providing comfort and restoration.

The good news is, I have a glorious story that is much more than purple!

With Me embraces the poetic essence of a God-directed life. Undoubtedly, you will see God has been with me through painful and joyful seasons. I have a loving family who has stood with me, trusted with me, and believed with me.

I have seen God unfurl His grace, and at other times He has simply asked: just be *With Me* and wait.

My prayer is that you will experience God's beauty in each expression and ask Christ for yourself: be with me.

"As for me, I will always have hope;
I will praise you more and more."

Psalm 71:14, NIV

With Me

Where have you gone, Lord?
Send help again!
A loved one, a kind word, the hand of a friend?
I need someone to walk closely alongside,
And though I don't want to hide,
I can't face this, one more day.
My bones grow weary, my mind drifts away.
Fragmented, tormented by what's left behind.
I kneel before You.
Be With Me, You whisper.
I hear your cry, I know your mind.
Don't lose hope, don't lose heart.
Your cares are untangled,
But I gathered them all,
Carrying them and you.
With Me,
Peace is restored.
With Me,
Prayer becomes song.
With Me,
Praise resounds, free.

Upside Down

This is the direction I am headed,
In this world, both familiar and foreign.
Do I actually remember what I did?
Where am I?
What day has begun?
Forget all convention,
Random facts, recollections.
There is nothing left to recall.
Everything has been erased,
Vanished, gone, untraced.
How can I wrap my mind around
Upside down?
A dimension unfound,
God, You are the Creator.
I know this is true.
Is my world upside down,
Or the one envisioned by You?

My Child

My child, I sing over you,
And I will never forsake you or let your foot fail.
Join with me, proclaim,
Rejoice in my Name.
My plan is perfectly crafted, beyond compare.
While delay may seem unending,
My heart deeply cares.
You are My child, called and redeemed,
And I Am here, faithful, beyond your best dream,
A comfort, a shelter through storms and through strife,
In mercy, restoring joy, giving hope to your life.

Life Is Ugly

Reality is, life can be ugly.
Storms will come, untamed and raw,
Leaving you no place to turn.
Walking with faith becomes reality,
When you need God to simply breathe.
Never waiver in the wind.
Darkness cannot win.
Choosing joy ushers in the boundless love
God gives,
For the unexpected times
When life is ugly.

Purple Overcomes Black

Black,
A darkness swirling in my mind, causing pain,
Awakened by a hue of purple,
Breaking through the black.
Purple,
The color of hope, of dawn creeping through the
    shadows,
Making way for light.
Black
Fights back.
Purple
Battles to win,
With warm shades of love, healing to wash away the
    black.
Purple,
Glorious color,
The royal robe of a King.
Black,
Swirling,
Causing pain.
Purple,
Shining,
The victorious ray of hope,
As purple overcomes black.

Until It Was Opened

With a choke hold on my neck,
I clenched my jaw,
Bearing the burden,
Losing the cherished joy.
Silence forgot the gift, locking it away,
Unheard.
Until the lock was opened
No one else knew the gift was sealed.
But then You spoke,
A beautiful surprise,
Releasing the choke hold,
Summoning a voice inside.
Refreshing water washed away tears as I lifted up to
You the gift,
Finding its joy in two songs of praise,
One voice to raise,
Dedicating this treasure to You,
For if it had never been locked away,
Endlessly closed,
I might not have remembered the beauty of rejoicing it
  enclosed.

The Ridge

Feet pound up the path at a thundering pace,
Fists clenched tightly, blocking blows intended to slow
  this race.
Twists, turns, but always uphill,
Trying to find the ridge that leads to the valley below.
A trek to find tranquility can be treacherous.
Inhale slowly, take a breath.
Footsteps locate the ridge of balance and rest,
Eyes gaze down on the valley,
Where peace is not a mirage but a reality.

Infiltrating

We didn't ask for this,
We couldn't see the curve in the road,
The crashes, the tears descended.
Fear knew no end.
We have a firm rock, always faithful, always present,
Even when darkness was heavy and unrepentant.
We never doubted You would keep the way safe,
Stirring up songs of joy, for peace to settle in this
  place.
Purple may have stained this life,
But the red of Your blood is the only color that
  matters,
Infiltrating with untarnished freedom.

Whistle

The tiny blue bird on the branch above me whistles a
   song of praise
For beauty that is given, even though it passes away,
And in her clear, little whistle,
Lifting praise to her Maker,
I hear joy floating through the air in a grateful way.

If Only

If only I could remember
Daily,
Where to put my treasure,
Trust,
For victory, to conquer with grace,
Belief,
For surrender, to let You win the race.
If only I could remember.

The Observer

An unexpected sight,
Crushed by the weight of what it contained, changed
  eternity.
The observer's heart fell through the rubble,
Too fast for him to chase.
Only he can see his memories now, scattered across
  the road,
Ones he cannot erase.
A Holy One's presence was there, amid the pain and
  trouble,
Observing and comforting those He called to serve in
  this position.
An impossible act of repairing cracks could only be
  done by His heroic act,
One Observer reaching down in love,
One observer reaching up, looking for mercy.
Restoring the heart with His almighty perfection,
The loving Observer allowed the observer's eyes once
  again to overflow with the gift he was given,
Giving love.

Answers

Nothing they can say,
No one knows what to do,
Each word only
Another voice in the wind.
Their attempts at answers
Prompt my own query:
What would happen if they knew You?

Unknown Prayer

Tears of sadness, tears of sympathy
On the cheeks of a valiant princess,
Praying for me, halfway around the world.
Whispering, pleading, kneeling,
Waging war for my healing,
Praying peace for my soul,
Unknown by me, yet not unnoticed by You,
Jehovah-Rapha.

Pure Joy

Tiptoes reach up in sheer delight,
One eye opened, one closed tightly.
Fingers grasp a long, white thread
That tethers joy at its end.
Joy is simple, pure and free,
Its laughter loud, ringing gleefully,
Floating higher and higher until toes lift in flight.
A purple balloon bobs up and down,
Dipping low to alight.
The source of joy, has it been found?
Or could it be, this joy we see
Is simply the happiness You have given as a reminder
That all You ask of us is to let go in childlike wonder?

Special

How do you stand in the middle of the line,
Quietly building your brilliant mind,
Shouting to be heard?
Eyes and lips quick to laugh,
Or, closer to the center,
Is it the tender heart that pulls people closer?
For without the middle,
There is no beginning or end.
That is, after all, what makes the middle special.

Not as Bad

"Not as bad" is a funny measure.
For us, it is a daily treasure,
Somewhere between heavy and light,
Between small strength and great might.
Our "not as bad" burden can never outweigh
Your sacrifice,
The load You bear on our behalf,
Knowing that our efforts could never suffice.
For Your goodness far exceeds our endeavors,
In full,
Never half.
So, we lay this measure at Your feet,
And in our "not as bad" there is no defeat.

The Curve

Intense,
Calculating,
Deliberate deception.
Dig in, blink once, deep breath, now deliver.
They won't see the seam coming as it breaks right,
  round, sinks down toward the dirt.
No need to look up, you know the pitch, you know
  the hurt.
Confident placement, the call goes for you.
A pound in the glove, another one down, nod the
  head, circle the mound.
Dig in once more,
Nod, blink and studied toss.
You knew it was there,
Umps have called it,
Other batters have been fooled
By that curve.

Sought Out

A warning,
A cry
A weary sigh.
You heard it and prayed,
Searched till you found me.
It was quite a day,
My lowest at best,
Until you sought me out,
Gave me comfort and rest.

Adapting

Adapting is wearisome,
As a soul weeps for hope
And each space between breaths seems an eternity.
Is there strength to endure?
Losses of dreams demand attention,
Trapping a heart from each direction.
Exhaustion and grief tempt to drown the very
   existence,
Leaving little rest to be found,
Trying not to lose sight of the bigger picture,
Where healing and hope become a fulfilling, adaptive
   mixture.

Highlight or Haunt

Highlight or Haunt,
Both battle for space inside.
Haunt is knocking to escape from the sun, waiting for
sunset to begin.
Colorful highlights, sweet hues of purples, blues and
greens,
Haunt cannot withstand.
Now fractured and crooked, Haunt is no longer a
fright,
Highlighted by yellow,
No longer locked up in me, chased out by the Light.

Beautiful You

Beautiful you, with so many hats to wear.
Four feathers broadcast delight:
Grace colors one,
Hope laces the others.
Trying on hats is no easy task,
Since there is always another on the rack.
The fondest of mine is brushed with kindness,
Drips with glitter, lets all colors of God's love shine,
Reflects Light, lavishes others with prayer and love,
Rising to the top, becoming my favorite.
The ageless collection grows,
Spreading beauty and joy as life's journey goes.

Little Sprite

Beauty that lies within you, freely toted around,
Wherever you go,
Flying through the door like a breath of fresh wind,
Overflowing with joy,
Drawing everyone in.
A little sprite dancing around in the sun,
Leaving sparkles wherever you've spun,
Fascinated by life.
With every turn in the Light,
Your gift of beauty shines outside and inside,
  undeniably bright.

Where Are Those Words

Where are those words,
Empty, never said,
Calloused and hollowed, filled with dread?
Where are those words that brought constant battles,
So unfair for a small one to bear?
Where are those words that longed to be heard,
Empty and meaningless, spilled on the floor.
You picked up those words, Lord, and gathered them
   in,
Pouring mercy and grace to the child within.
Words now given back, thankfully found,
Saying, "I love you,"
Forever and more.

Embrace

Embrace this moment,
Let love wrap around,
Simply let go and ponder
The God of wonder.
Willingly lean into the arms of His embrace,
The One who stepped down from His throne,
   showing mercy and grace.
Realize this moment was created for you,
A time appointed, He knew.
So, embrace it, make it your own:
Run, dance, simply let go.

Nothing to Give

They tell me you did your best,
A mantra I detest.
Angry words, empty eyes,
Mountains of lies.
My world lay twisted and jarred,
A child's cries.
If you had so much to give,
How could you let me slip away?
Split in two,
Only one side pursued.
Nothing to give—that was your best.
Thankfully, a Savior showed what value I hold,
Seeing me through loving eyes,
Silencing my cries,
For all was not lost,
As He gave something better, on the cross.

Tea

Can the simple act of ordering tea
Make me wonder who I'm meant to be?
A safe bet,
Always the same so as not to fret.
No one sees the me, the me I see,
In the secret way I order tea.

Losing Touch

It is cloudy out today,
In a rainy, foggy sort of way,
With miles and miles of haze ahead.
When will this journey end?
Memories, like dreams, are not always delightful.
Looking back is twice as frightful,
Mingled with fog and despair,
Disorienting in this thick, wet air,
For it is cloudy out today.
Between what I see and what I dream,
Will you be waiting there?
To help dispel a nagging fear
Of something I cannot possibly define,
It is cloudy in my mind.

Overwhelmed

Overwhelmed by glory,
Yet not understanding Your message of "holy."
Veiled in brilliance beyond our dreams,
Holy is pure, holy is Christ,
A value not to ascribe or attain,
Rather, appointed,
Anointed.
The King of Glory, pure and holy,
Reaching down with beauty and love to a tainted
   world.
Holy cannot be understood or felt.
It is enough to express
Whispered adoration.
There is but One most worthy
Of the truth, the call of holy,
The Lord, the Three in One.

Yellow Petals

Bound together by bright yellow petals once stretched
    tall to the sun,
Petals now trampled, disregarded on the ground.
We need one another to pick up the petals, find life
    somehow,
Offer prayers for the sun to shine.
You left a surprising gift amid the pain of fallen petals,
Seeds of hope that will climb ahead,
Finding rays of sunshine, redemption instead of dread,
Full of vibrant color, kissed by the sun,
Filling the fields with a brilliant yellow harvest,
Where we find ourselves bound together again in love.

Do You Remember

Do you remember the day we let go,
Hesitant, trusting God with both hands?
You slid away quickly,
Out of our view for a quick breath,
Falling or flying—it was hard to decide.
There is beauty in growing, learning how to slide,
Knowing we are the ones who remember
The day we let go.

Thorn

There are two sides to this thorn—
One is seen, the other worn,
As pain forced into silence
By eyes that only want to walk by and ignore it.
You feel the pain of barbs—You have born,
Much longer and deeper,
Bloodshed, a crown worn.
I can live with this thorn if that's what You choose,
Gaining new perspective, pointed views.
Help me never forget, as I go on my way,
To see this thorn as a gift
To bear with peace, dignity and grace.

Mother Heart

Did desperation sear through your heart,
Watching the wretched road your son walked?
Longing to save him from the pain,
Your mother heart, filled with grief and disdain,
Was desperate for a glimpse, from him to you,
Yet knowing this was what you were born to do.
What words could be spoken to your Mother heart,
Whispers of love to encourage,
To answer every anguished prayer,
Did your Mother heart scoop up every drop of blood
    that flowed down from your Holy Son,
Mingled with tears of love?
His promises, etched in the cross, still resound,
And as He sees your Mother heart, He remembers.

Alone

Left alone in the cleft of a rock,
All I could do was hide,
Pull a blanket over my head and have a good cry,
Unable to answer the question of why.
You reminded my soul that the most beautiful songs
  of praise
Were faithfully written on days much like mine,
By one in the royal blood line.
Thankful to remember Your Word in my heart,
I uncovered my head and started to walk
In the miracle of praise sustaining me.

Caught Off Guard

An escape for them,
None for us.
Here, can you take it?
We need to run.
Cast away to the side,
It's your fault, you see.
You never really knew what was to be,
But our plan was to never let you escape from their
    view,
In silence,
Abandoned.
They cast their net deep,
Caught off guard by You.

Identity

I wonder What my identity would be if You had not
   found me.
The gift to the child is to have no memory of loss.
I wonder Who my identity would be if You had not
   found me.
Gone, erased? A name changed, just a face?
I wonder Where my identity would be if You had not
   found me.
Would it be misplaced or filled with grace?
I wonder What my identity would be if You had not
   found me.
I know it would be grafted to You,
For You are the One who saw the plan through.

Purple Day

This endeavor to encapsulate results in isolation.
No one really sees the fight, despite your good
   intentions.
Faces, names, events fall short.
They cannot possibly reinforce
The reality of what you hope to endorse.
Pictures of small victories
Seem invalid and less empowering.
Just like numbers, struggles truly never end.
There is no measure to apply,
Showing, once again,
That isolation
Will always have a qualification.

Grace

Grace is a path through the way of the unknown,
Not merely spoken or bestowed,
There to be found when walls close in tightly,
Like a grip on the heart that makes the soul ache.
Search for grace,
Make it your own,
For the path laced with grace
Will shoulder your burden and lead you home.

Breath

While there is breath,
I will follow with blind faith,
Praying for a last-minute miracle to show its face,
Believing and breathing prayers of restoration,
For life-giving breath is the nature of your
  foundation.

Mother Tears

The tears of a Mother fall forever,
Dropping on embers to douse the flame.
Intuition guiding, knowing,
Her heart overflowing.
A gut-wrenching silence cries from within her,
Tears that only a Mother can shed for another
Pour out over and over again to console.

Ode to the Missing

Where did he go?
Do people remember
A brother, a son, a loved one who mattered?
Where is the sadness, mourning for lost life?
I wonder whatever became of his heart.
He was funny and smart,
Misunderstood.
Did anyone help him, the way Christians should?
Memories fade, drift away,
While clinging to hope that he was restored.
Where did he go? Why didn't he stay?
His life deserved more.

Hands Off

Hands off,
He is taken,
Sealed by the blood of Christ,
Redeemed, claimed, forgiven.
The line is drawn.
Plain to see,
Victory sealed.
Hands off,
His life is won.

Stories Told

Stories told,
Dreams wished,
Some left unfulfilled.
Reality of life quickly unfolds,
Gone in a moment, other stories untold.
You taught in parables, keepsakes now past
And present.
From beginning to end,
You placed red letters that last,
Gifts for a lifetime.
Yet the end of the tale
Awaits fulfillment as another page draws near,
Glorious splendor still to appear.

The Faithful

I am not surprised by the work You have done,
Merciful, mighty,
You've overcome.
I am not surprised,
Because I have learned to believe
What only You can achieve.
Faith's stories stand tall,
Flourishing from wells of deep faith,
Proclaiming that Your promises are true,
And evermore thankful today, I can call on You.

Unexpected

That day things turned out unexpectedly, so wrong.
It just didn't follow the plan I had all along.
If Your Word is true, then why was this happening?
Shocked, astonished, lonely,
This wasn't how it was supposed to be.
It should have been a safe place for me.
What had I done?
Life changed in an instant, plummeting, profound.
You stood by my side as I laid my heart down,
Trusting the unseen, what was yet to be revealed,
Knowing that Your Word is true, spiritually sealed,
A Rock of love,
Covering, sheltering, protecting,
While I learn to expect Your love to show up at times
   unexpectedly.

Eye Level

The street was grey, just about eye level,
Fingers curled slowly over the ledge so eyes could see
  better.
Sounds were quiet and loud, all at once.
I stood and watched for quite a long time,
Seeing brilliance just beyond my view.
A parade passed by, splendid indeed,
And then, scrutinizing with my eyes was no longer a
  need.
Jumping over the wall, I yelled, "Wait for me!"
That's when my eye level changed, coming eye to eye
  with My Savior, My King,
On streets paved with gold,
A new perspective
Brought to eye level.

Remember

You can't run, you can't hide,
From the hollowness inside.
It pounds on your chest,
Deep down, no rest,
Grips your soul, rips you up, lays you flat.
You can't run, you can't hide or turn back.
Escape is on the other side.
You've been there before, so why not continue to
    try?
"Remember" cries out, as you go down once more.
This time, you struggle and pull yourself off the
    floor.
Strength fills your lungs with power.
This is your day.
You can run, you won't hide.
You will cross the line as a victor this time.

Rushing Wind

Oh, rushing wind, wild and untamed,
Capture my soul, run through my veins,
Push me, throw me,
Show me your ways,
Blow through these caverns, cold, dark enclaves.
Dry winds, rush over, roar loud,
Shout redeemed!
Move the clay turned to dust,
Clear the path, create a course.
This mighty wind is fierce, moving fast,
Caught up, turned over.
Let this be the last.
Oh, mighty wind, wash over me,
Whisper Your love in a soft, gentle breeze.

Forward I

Leading,
Marching, onward, forward,
From the front a place to go.
Flowing swiftly,
With motion unceasing,
Forceful waves push forth the flow.
Thinking,
Never looking back,
Eyes ahead
Guarding to direct the path,
Pulled ahead
By the One above
Who forged the way forward,
With passion and love.

Forward II

Leaving behind,
Moving on,
Painful steps.
Regrets or not, there's no turning back.
An uphill climb,
Not an easy task to ask.
Share the load,
Give it away.
If it is two steps ahead, one step back,
Forward is still where you will always track.

Forward III

How far will I continue to sink,
Until I turn my thoughts around?
Beauty surrounds me,
Sweet fragrance abounds.
Shake off the ties that have held me tightly,
A past laden with words, bitter, unsightly.
Take hold, my soul, in the Lord most High,
The One who broke chains of death and redeemed my
  mind.

Forward IV

Is it a sleight of hand
That makes a triangle slip through the circle in a
   magician's hand?
The tip must be cracked, surely interlocking shape
   upon shape,
Geometric patterns blurred and merged into one
   landscape.
Bound now simply by your fight,
How does this affect your sight
Of what the Master can do for you?
The link could be open in one quick move.
Let Him show you His forgiveness,
Unbound and free.
The pattern can be broken.
Bolster your existence,
Move forward without resistance.

Overflowing

She set the tea for two.
A prayer spoken, then chats more casual,
And soon, I noticed something new:
One cup was overflowing.
As she sipped, she talked of grace,
How thankful we could be
For everything from tea to bread,
Herbal aroma, sweet spread,
And most abundantly,
Unwavering love from You.
Her tea kept flowing, pouring into me,
Grateful for this time of humble overflowing,
Sharing Your kindness through the act of setting tea.

Almighty God

Glorious and holy,
Almighty God,
What can ever express gratitude,
Right now,
Right here?
For what You have given is so much more,
Than what I could ever have dreamed then,
Than what I could ever have hoped back there,
And so, I utter feeble and yet heartfelt thanks
To You, Almighty God.

Poured Out

Hope resurrected
Ran after the one, chased him down.
Rejoice:
Lost is found.
Then, ripples and waves of tears below
Mingle with resounding, glorious praises above,
As souls are snatched back to Your heavenly love.
After my weeping and gasping,
I remain, asking,
How do these lost ones come to Your side?
Soon, answered prayers tell me:
I know what you have done,
Pouring out Your love for just one.

Shadows

Shadows dance across the wall,
Going on walks,
Dropping to the floor.
Shadows follow down the hall,
Making it hard to step or shut the door
Closed.
Open the Book, and a shadow still falls,
Until bright light shines down,
Erasing shadows through the gleaming Son,
His glory
Exposed.

Weariness

Will I rest my weary mind,
Leave the cares and just unwind?
The pain is deep, it hurts to turn.
As I wrestle side to side,
Memories creep into my back,
Up my spine.
The headache, the heartache,
With every shallow breath I take.
Jehovah-Rapha, take my hand,
Guide me through a restless land,
Healing, peace and restfulness,
Where weariness does not exist.

How Can We Show You

How can we show you our love,
Except through the One whose expression of love
Exceeds our imagination?
From your very beginning, God was present,
Wrapping our gift in the protection of His promise.
When times were uncertain,
We stood on God's plan,
Always trusting that His words
For you
Are true.
We walked along the narrow path,
The uncharted road,
Drawing on strength only Heaven could unload.
Our gift from God,
Answer to prayer,
How can we show you our love?
The only way we know how.
Sharing stories of the Creator
Ours and yours,
Knowing that His great faithfulness is perfectly
Packaged in this gift called—you.

You Will Be Me

You will be me someday,
The one standing afar,
Looking on for a piece of who you thought you were.
Your memories aren't entangled with theirs,
Not even the same.
Harsh realities deny even your name.
Don't close your eyes on your beauty and grace,
For you get to be me someday.
There is One holding a place,
Standing afar,
Staying near.
Seek Him out,
Run to Him.
He will be there,
Ready to show you that we need not fear.

Tic-Toc, Tic I

A very loud clock calls out the time—
Tic-Toc, Tic-Toc—and then it chimes,
Drawing attention, demanding to be heard.
It is exacting, Tic-Toc can trap in a second,
A hazard
Occupying our minds, minute by minute.
Holding us captive in time, Tic-Toc is continually
   stalking.
Freedom from noise requires seeking
What lies between the lines
The Word of God reveals.
His presence in life is sound,
Not requiring the Tic-Toc, Tic-Toc to keep on talking.
Live beyond time, don't be bound by the present.

Tic-Toc, Tic II

Tic-Toc inside my heart.
Who stands with me and what sets me apart?
Listen carefully that Tic-Toc doesn't haunt the places
  you go,
Haunt your dreams driven by mockery.
Tic-Toc inside my mind.
Will time run out, will time unwind?
Stop the clock from chiming,
Cry out against the alluring song,
Block the clock,
From being the
Tic-Toc inside my dreams.

Beauty

Beauty is only fleeting at best,
Surrounding
In the wind and the sea,
And yet it can be
Restored,
Given new life,
Like the beautiful mess
Of the Lamb's sacrifice,
A staggering price,
Offering redemption,
Restoring beauty's intention,
As the Lamb felt great pain,
While bearing our shame
So that beauty could be complete
Beauty.

My Gift

My gift is precise,
Mathematically correct.
Its corners align, engineered perfectly,
Crafted carefully
By hands who envisioned a purpose.
Balanced, held together with love.
Calculated beyond what I could have designed,
My gift now sits on display with units of measure.
Not wanting to break a treasured gift could be
   wrong,
But watching it teaches me to remember the love
It sums up and multiplies,
Rather than reducing it to an ordinary exercise.

Four Chambers

There are four chambers in the heart, pumping life-
   giving blood,
And while three are filled by Father, Son and the Holy
   One,
The fourth chamber stands open for you or me
To work with the perfect Trinity,
Only if we ask God in, receiving life's blood source, the
   redeeming plan.
Protecting it,
Guarding it,
Working as one,
Our heart beats in unison,
Sharing sounds of extraordinary love.
When seemingly the chambers cease to give life,
We immediately appear before glorious light,
The heart of the Father's face,
Where we see the extent of blood spilled at the cross
   by our Lord Jesus Christ,
An eternal heartbeat of life.

How Long Must I Wait

How long must I wait?
Is that what they thought as they sat at the gate,
Or was it easy to keep eyes on You,
Humming humble praises and psalms?
If they walked so closely with You,
Did time matter while they waited to finally behold?
Standing on Your Word was enough.
Oh, might I learn how to trust You that much,
With every fiber of being, no matter how long
I feel stretched,
My feet standing firm,
Eyes focused only on You and Your Word.

Rise

This rise will not be quiet,
For sound cannot be contained,
Like flowers bursting forth in glory
From dreary seeds of winter pain.
While thundering rain
May pour down,
With hail and mighty power,
New life and beauty cannot be crushed,
Merely refreshed
By rain from the heavens.
The third day was not quiet,
As Christ shook off His linen shroud.
The Lion roared,
Life restored,
In glorious rounds of praise.
This rise will not be quiet,
The Messiah's great return,
When bones arise, break open graves,
No longer bound by earthly chains.
Heaven's sounds will not be contained,
As the skies are opened wide
In victory, deafening,
With Christ's trumpet call beckoning,
A final rise that reigns
Forevermore.

Look Up

Heralded in glory,
Eyes drawn to the sky,
To find the shining light that marked our Savior's cry.
Hallelujah! Hallelujah!
A perfect Lamb has come,
So let us, let me,
Look up to find the news of the promised Holy One.
Draw my eyes to You, Lord,
To focus on Your Name,
Attach my soul, that I might, too,
Look up in awe as the night when angels sang.

Purple Hope

One stumble,
A mistake in time,
As purple hope crumbles.
Why now,
Why this time for me to remember?
Thunderous waves crash loudly,
Hope feels lost along the shoreline,
Littered and mingled among life's purple battles.
When the tide recedes,
Your Word is all that I see,
For You really never left me.
Salty tears,
Shed in fear,
Are wiped away,
Reflecting Your strength accumulated throughout the
    years.
Oh, faithful Redeemer, forgive me,
And I won't be washed away as the sand pulls out.
Secure in Your Word,
My purple hope will not doubt.

The Patient Listener

The words that circle within my mind
Go faster and faster, a tornado inside,
Bouncing back and forth, often nonsensical.
My eyes read them sharply, darting past,
Hoping they are not incomprehensible,
And whirling continues until I shout, "Cease!"
One breath in, one breath out,
Words still roll about.
Do they hear me continue to slow,
Telling the story they want you to know?
It's not always easy,
The words are all jumbled,
From the twirling that circled inside my head.
But I have found a patient listener,
Never a judge,
Who pours out His love,
As Creator of the mind where the words beautifully
   dwell.

Digging Deep

I want to hide away.
Where do I weep?
Deep in my soul,
Beyond where I think.
If I dig into Your Word,
Will I find a hole too deep,
Or one not deep enough to hold the pain?
Should I just keep digging deep,
Or lay down at Your feet?

Give Me Grace

If I've lost your face,
Please give me grace.
I might not remember the time or the place
That we once passed through the same space.

Eyes On You

Eyes always on You,
Watching each move.
Really, what do they expect of the view?
An up-close inspection
To start and end the day.
The rounded, reflective rim they use
Distorts the view, this one they choose.
It leaves me fragile, alone, confused.
Give me strength to deflect the stares,
Remembering that I live this one life
To glorify You.

Searching for Sleep

Lord, I'm tired tonight.
Help me sleep,
Avoid dreams that make me weep.
Cast my mind aside,
Remind me that in You I abide.
Sweet peace, promises are certain to keep,
And You alone will refresh my soul.
Draw me to Your side,
Allow me to circumvent the noise,
Give me slumber, a place to hide.

The Rock I

How do you open your eyes?
In a confusion of shadows, panic swirling inside your
   head,
Tears stream down, brimming with dread.
How do you choose to stand without crumbling
Having the courage to explore the core of spiritual
   troubles?
I know a Rock to lean on, a beacon of hope in a
   world gone astray.
He withstands any burden you want to give away.

The Rock II

Passion and grief,
You have walked our ways,
Choosing suffering with joy,
Providing healing through the pain.
A rock to stand on, magnificent to ponder,
Your graciousness despite our floundering and
    proneness to wander.
Must You show me Your hands and feet once again,
So that I can believe healing is possible?
Throw off my doubting Thomas' heart,
Let me see the passion endured through grief.
My Rock, the call You gladly heard.

The Rock III

Too much to bear alone,
Wrapped in a blanket to ward off the chill,
A foundation of love built over the years.
A Rock ever present, catch our tears,
Pleading still
Upon Your faithful ears,
Willing life into bones,
Mercy for minutes left here on Earth.
Cling to the Rock who makes nightmares quake,
Desperately believing our Savior's Cross will
    intervene,
Sparing loss and relieving our pain.

Passing Over

Aaron and David, in line of Priest and King,
Tragedy knew their names,
Grief each father felt in loss of sons, must have been
  the same,
Ancestors familiar with cries of firstborn sons taken,
But for the blood shed by a lamb spared their homes,
  left unshaken.
Your only Son also surrendered,
Great High Priest, King of Kings,
Perfect Passover Lamb shedding His blood,
Knowing separation and darkness.
The heart of a father is not lost,
So, we can hand over our sorrow and pain at the
  grave,
Trading broken hearts for joy, knowing we will see
Your face one day.

Umbrella

Have I become calloused by pain,
Jaded by rain
That continues to fall in puddles?
I would put up an umbrella
If I thought it would protect me from the persisting
  floods.
Hiding from just one drop could be enough.
If I chose to defer to a man-made invention,
Would I miss the joy of feeling
Satisfaction and healing,
Through Your miraculous intervention?

Reflection

A single ripple rolled across the undisturbed surface,
Inviting me to walk closer, with purpose.
What lay beneath was surprising to me,
Mesmerized by its beauty now washed back, to see
A reflection,
Not the one I expected to appear,
For all of a sudden, You were mirrored there.
Time was lost as I took in Your presence,
Reflecting on how You have saved me by grace in
    reverence.
Quietly another wave rolled across the surface,
Showing me what I was meant to see all along,
A reflection of You mirrored in me,
On a surface of serenity.

Looking Back

Looking back is not always easy.
Places linger in your mind,
Memories are a cinematic glimpse, though less
  refined.
A place to go, not a place to behold.
Turning around to look ahead,
The memory I want to count as gold.

Denial

I despise denial, the pain it caused,
I despise denial, the time it took away.
The shell encased a beauty you hide,
Crushing blows, spitting out terror deep inside.
How could this beauty go unseen, just disappear
Into confusion, doubt and lies self-taught?
Hard work and prayer are required to conquer this
  hold.
I despise denial, it was empty and cold,
Until a saving Light arose, resetting a heart's path,
Making it right,
Reshaping sight
With bountiful beauty and delight.

Caution

Caution is part of pain,
An emotion not many experience at all.
Not one that looks to the left or the right,
Caution grabs the mind, holds tight,
Decides on its own who will win.
Each step taken sends caution to flight,
Stealing bravery known only to those who must
  fight.
Caution turns to fear, if not contained,
Paralyzing, criticizing, calling a name.
Turning to You is the only escape,
Allowing caution to leave through Your Holy Gate,
Where the pathway to peace is steady and straight.

Hope and Storm

Hope is easily forgotten in the middle of a storm.
Renewing the mind is renewing the soul.
What if hope relies on renewal
For the very fact of finding hope and healing?
Christ, the Creator, the giver of hope,
Remind me to find You each time I wake up.
Whenever a storm has rattled my mind,
I will stand firm in belief.
Hope will settle in my heart and heal the battle I fight,
Overcoming a storm,
Rising in Your resurrection.

Cast Your Net

You cast Your net on the stormy sea,
Opening wide Your arms to rescue me.
You walked the waves to pull me out,
Pouring love, replacing doubt.
In turn, You ask that I fish for more,
Return the net, bring it to shore,
Promising a place with You of eternal bliss,
A once stormy sea, now glistening clear with life, as
   with fish.

Please Remember

For a while, some remember the pain of alone.
Isolation for them was quite unknown.
Reimagining a life, not a task they must face.
Taking it on ourselves makes it easy to disappear and
   embrace,
Fading from the minds of people once trusted,
Routines lost, just now adjusted.
Reach out with God's love—
That's all we ask.
After all, isn't that simply what was tasked
To us by Jesus?
Reimagine life with me,
Where we walk through change faithfully,
Not forgotten or defeated by isolation,
Only rejoicing in this situation.

Mingled

There is no why,
Just Your way,
What You have to say.
Covenant faithful, keeper of time,
Then and now, Lord, I stand with You,
That you might mingle my whys into Yours.

Surely

My mind is filled with voices crying,
Holy God, why am I falling?
Life and purpose, deep despair
Leave my eyes beyond repair.
Surely, since You are a God who cares,
I only need Your shadow to find rest,
Just a hem of Your vest,
Casting holiness.
Righteous judge, I cannot escape,
So, show me the path I should take,
Bring my mind home to rest in Your embrace,
Secure in knowing Your peace can never be replaced.

How?

How can I possibly sit here and enjoy the beauty
Of what I see,
When the plight of humanity
I know cries out,
And dies in doubt
Of Your love for them and for me?

Rescue

Make them steadfast, sure and true,
In spite of what they see from You.
Weeping, turn to joy, I beg.
Help them escape the captor's dread.
Why is suffering their call,
When Your gift of love is for us all?
I cry out in a desperate plea:
Rescue, restore, protect those in need,
Spread word of Your hope through what they endure,
Knowing victory in Heaven is secured.

Show Me

Shame on me for falling short.
Have I not prayed, sought Your heart?
Now I know,
I have seen the facts.
How can I turn my back?
If prayer touches eternity,
Then may my heart be entwined with all that You
   see,
Lifting indebted praise and prayer.
Show me my place in healing this land.

Lost Girl

Eyes closed tight, dare she dream
Of an existence in a world that has forgotten her
  quiet scream?
Is there hope in this impossible scheme?
Fixing the improbable remains Your mission:
Parting the Red Sea, raising the dead were not stories
  of fiction.
She needs Your reliable presence now,
So, shelter her and show her how
You are her cloud by day, fire by night,
A never-ending guiding light.

Rows of Bones

A peculiar view through a hole in the stone,
Looking over rows of bones
Who face a lush valley of greens teeming with life,
As if knowing they will one day be heralded out,
Walking freely with You, Jesus Christ.

Ein Gedi

Swirls of green and purple,
Scents of lavender fill the room,
The source, one piece of the land You love—an
  enticing perfume.
Drawn to the beauty are hands covered in dust,
  needing purification,
Lathered and rinsed, all signs of grime washed away,
No longer to be remembered,
Only the sweet fragrance of Ein Gedi.

The Gate

The gate is small, it is not wide,
Barely big enough to see inside.
My eyes behold a glorious view—
Will I catch a glimpse as Your chosen walk through?
Knowing the thrill that awaits
Makes me ever grateful for this gate,
Where I can simply sit in wonder to ponder my own
  fate.

It Is Said

It is said, You sailed across a sea to find a bit of rest.
Feeding hungry souls brings weariness.
It is said, You journeyed across deserts and
  mountains
To teach and heal the sick.
It is said, You knew and experienced the pain of
  humanity,
Trials beyond compare, compelled exhaustion from the
  cross You bore.
If this is true, then surely You feel the anguish that
  lives within me,
Worn out from another round of battling epilepsy.
It is said, You rose again, conquered death and pain,
Reassurance of hope,
Knowing You understand what I'm going through.

Tomb of Bones

Burned in stone, piles on piles,
Lie markers of memories forgotten in sorrow.
Peering through this arch allows a beautiful view
To the valley below, its peace almost too quiet to be
    true.
My eyes keep watch, not growing weary,
Waiting in silence for just one to move.
Your Word is poetic, precious and true,
Valued by those who truly know You.
You've raised bones to life,
You'll do it again.
A crystal blast from Your trumpet will call forth these
    bones,
Riddled now with decay.
I do not want to miss it, I'm determined to catch
A glimpse of how brilliant and glorious it will be,
When bones shaking off dust to return to their
    Maker,
Viewing Your kingdom come,
Your will be done
With Your earthly creations.

The Statue

Statuesque, copper, making landscape magnificent,
Telling the story, carved, reaching out,
But in my mind, doubts rolled about.
A statue is not the Christ we know,
The one who is alive and moving,
His outstretched arm not stopping midair,
Despite the monument planted there.
Jesus gathers children close,
Active motion, sweeping in the very ones He loves
   the most.
Little ones who touch His heart,
Not stopped beneath a solid, cold piece of art.

Empty Tomb

"It is empty," they said,
Eyes troubled with fright,
For their Savior had just been placed there last night.
A cold empty tomb was all they could see,
And with spices in hand, there was no longer a need,
With the stone rolled away, no body lay dead.
Glorious angels proclaimed, "He has risen!"
Quickly they ran to spread their delight:
Jesus lives, He has given us life!

Buckets

Do tears fill up buckets with the cries of a nation,
Forced to watch horrors untold while the world turns a
  blind eye in isolation?
Do they wonder where You are,
Left rotting away, feeling their very existence slipping
  into a pitiful basin?
Who brings them hope,
Who brings them courage?
Are my knees bending in prayer or standing in quiet
  ignoration?
Martyrs sacrificing their blood for Your nail-scarred
  hands
Walk with them, and I must understand every pain
  they have.
Give me insight in some small way,
To show a nation, each person,
How the great I Am has not forgotten.

Awkward

Confusion appears on your face,
While blood drains from mine, makes my heart race.
Clearly my language has been jumbled at a disordered
   pace,
Awkward at best.
You can pass by, I understand,
But if you would stop, if you would stay,
We might both see this awkwardness
Become a moment of grace.

Trying to Talk

Did this sentence stop?
Did I say it again,
Perhaps over and over without an end,
Or did I start it again?
Oh, you said I skipped a word.
I think it best to put a stop to this thought I began.

Where Can I Hide

There's a place deep inside where I know I can hide.
Close my eyes, and it is moments away.
Quiet and dark, so I can't feel the hurt.
How I cope with the pain.
Please don't talk to me when I've crawled deep
  within.
My mind only handles so much as it is.
Let me curl up and focus on finding the center,
Until I can decide to surrender,
Finding the One who can light the dark.
I want to listen in silence as He speaks to my heart and
  says—
Whenever you want to open your eyes, it's OK,
I'll be waiting again to help you find your way.

Open the Page

It will just take a moment to open a page,
Learn something new,
Find direction as the day moves.
Open another, look further with care,
Examine Who made the Earth we share,
Created by One, yet uniquely different,
Planned from the start of life's very existence.
One moment more, love drawn on the page.
Let hope draw you in, deeply engage.

I Am Loved

Don't you know I am loved,
Even if not by your plan?
There is One who holds me in His almighty hand.
I am not a complication to Him,
Nor a remnant of sin.
He has never complained about my existence.
I am counted as one of His dearest.
Please stop continuing to make my heart ache.
Telling lies is an easy escape.
He's had an intention for me from the beginning of
   time.
Maybe you are the one who needs to refine
   definitions of complications,
Because God's love has no limitations.

Doors

It was a quiet, hopeful morning,
Anticipation was soaring,
Freedom, answers,
Our time to win.
Steady, sure, we held hands tightly,
As we always have through this fight.
We brushed lips lightly,
Smiles of confidence, see you soon, understood,
Then doors stepped in, to separate me from you.
Nothing went right.
Life dark as night.
Awakening sharply to bright lights and my love's
    tears filled with fear,
I once more disappeared.
I do not remember when life took a turn,
Only grateful for the chance to return,
To remember how precious it is to hold hands,
And to linger in each kiss like you might not return.

Sit With Me

Just lay with me and hold my hand,
As my mind wanders through drifting lands,
Never knowing when end is in sight.
Once it embarks on a derailing fright,
It circles back and round again.
Let me hold tight to your hand,
Sit with me for just a while,
Till I remember that I can smile.
Chase away the memory of loss,
Tell me I am not a lost cause.
Remind me of our ever-present Lord,
Who once again sent angels to surround us,
Always protecting, showing kindness.

Compartment

In a compartment,
That's where they are kept,
Memories of sickness, memories of death.
Each one, a picture, returns with a flash,
If I linger too long or dwell in the past.
No time for that now. I must move on.
The next one desperately deserves its own turn,
Before another memory is formed,
Locked in a compartment.
Focused, allowing myself freedom to move like a
    dance to a song,
Seamless rhythm, so smooth.
Life needs to win,
Joy must succeed, lest anyone see
My compartment filling up,
Wishing You would take the key.

The Little Things

It's the little things that make my tears fall for you.
Who else understands what we've been through,
Guiding as best you knew?
Memories pass like shadows across my eyes,
Quickly grabbing my attention, tricks and spies,
Sights of you for my soul to behold.
It will always be the little things that remind me of
  you,
Whenever the sun rises or sets.
It's OK to feel a tear run down in kind,
Reminding me you can be found in the little things of
  life.

Grateful for Joy

Grateful for joy in You,
More than I ever expected.
Seasons that should have been littered with pain
Continued to point to victory in your grave with
   every gain.
Joy in lessons along a path, bumpy, long and curved.
Drawing strength upon Your Word, we endured.
Hope is joyful, a sweet delight,
Needed when weary bones have no fight.
Grateful for joy, Mighty King,
Let us turn to You always,
With joy more than anything.

I Will Listen

I've never walked this road of heartache proposed to
   your mind now,
This level of a mother's loss,
Overwhelming sadness and questioning why.
Torrents of rain need
To fall on seeds,
To replace this madness. I will listen,
I will encourage.
I cannot bear this weary load.
All I know to say right now— Jesus is enough,
More than all we need.
I will stand with you until we see the fruit from
   seeds.

Number

What is a number that fills up a hand?
Feels like love when you see it waving furiously, fast
   and grand,
Reaches for yours to break a fall,
Yet seems so very small.
That one special number comes around once in a
   lifetime,
Wrapping around swings,
Soaring higher as they cling,
Carries buckets of sand from the sea,
Enables butterflies to be caught with ease.
That one special number dances freely,
Lifting praise to the Creator who made her.
Behold how this number fills the palm of your hand,
Trusting your wisdom, guiding her through God's
   plan.
Grip tightly this number—you'll never want to let go,
Knowing when you do, it will never come home.
Let this one special number cover your heart.
Numbers grow bigger, memories short.

Writer Beware

Words hurt, don't forget,
Built on love or in despair.
Others are profoundly impacted by letters that
    appear,
Not just the sounds,
But also shapes.
Writer beware,
A heart always aches by what is read,
Deeply felt as the day it was penned.

Ashes

Do not ask me to look on with delight.
My ashes burn in the pile where you hope to bury
  yours in plain sight.
Ashes burn my skin,
Leave traces of embers, smoldering thin.
Strewn across my life, residue spreads over places you
  cannot see.
Fiery coals mock beauty left within,
Dust reigns down without mercy,
Crimson coals alight, flickering shades of hope
  among grey ash, tossed about
A resurrection garden,
Replacing ashes for pardon.

Trees

Listen to the trees, they cry out "Hallelujah" as they
   rise,
Towering heights on either side.
Amid the forest, not one rock or creature can resist,
Shouting forth splendor, their God-given gift.
Warm days, cool nights,
A symphony ignites,
Choruses led by flora and fauna.
Moonbeams dance, leaving shimmering light
Reflected by the stars You left to guide.
A masterpiece cannot be denied.
Ripples and folds, valleys and hills,
Gently enveloped into the palm of Your hands.
As they fulfill what You ordained in Your will.

Why Fear

What do I have to fear?
You are at my door,
Knocking, knocking, drawing near,
Holding me in Your arms,
Rocking me to sleep.
Why should I fear when I know
Your promise of glory is clear?

Puzzle Piece

Four corners found, foundation laid.
Round the edge a frame was made.
Scattered all around the floor,
Thirty pieces, maybe more,
All of crooked size and shape.
Quickly they fell into place,
Until there was an open space,
Unmistakably displaced.
This is how I feel my mind,
A puzzle with a piece disinclined
To fill its spot or find a space,
So, I wander around continually in search
Of this missing piece to be unearthed.

Wedding

A day for dreams,
Hope and promise.
Birds chirp loudly in their given chorus,
Leaves resound in glorious shades of greens,
Sunlight dances across in flashing beams,
Preparing to display Your complete gift of love.
A three-stranded cord cannot easily be undone.
Slow down, look around:
The spectacle is grand,
Nature has given all to your hands,
So shall you two on this promise of days,
Give your hands to serve each other in magnificent
   ways.
Hold tight to this joy,
Draw from its strength,
With God's beauty and grace all around,
Offering hope to remember where love was found.

Ablaze

The light You hung in the heavens guides the way by
   day,
Ablaze on the horizon, fiery bright,
Causing me to hide, blinding my sight.
Moses could not look upon Your face,
In view of Your illuminating glory.
All will stand on Holy Ground,
As our forefathers, bowing before Your mighty
   presence,
Ablaze in power, almighty omnipotence,
Far more spectacular than a fiery sun,
Setting behind me as I turn to catch the last glimpse of
   its glory,
Watching it slip slowly away,
Yearning yet for You to set a fire ablaze in me.

Cards (Fifty-Two)

A deck of cards, fifty-two,
That's what it takes to play the hand you were dealt.
Nobody said life would be just or true,
What suite you will play to level the field,
Choices to yield or hit once more.
Exalt the thought,
To believe in what you've got.
Diamonds have suited you well in the past,
Throwing them all, chasing dreams that can't last.
Will you call, show your move?
Admit life's fact: you might lose.
Spades got you in the end.
You should have examined your hand,
Before you played all fifty-two.

Still Waiting

How I wish I could see answers of prayers cried out
  from generations long ago.
Help me understand mysteries in plans You have yet
  to show,
Connect the dots of Your faithfulness,
Directions only You know.
Reassurance is my quest,
Promises I long to put to rest.
Your covenant, everlasting,
Will keep godly words onward passing.
Carry whispered prayers of hope from generations
  who are still waiting
To greet their prayers in Heaven.

If Perhaps

Would I have rather known the end,
Or withered from the shell within?
Sit back, watch Your plan unfold,
Let contentment flow from the start of this road.
Life's winter might be cold and dark,
History is a lesson taught,
Showing many ways to walk.
Bible heroes trusting You, seem so clear.
Imagine perhaps—
The Israelites might not have left if they had known
   the wandering path
Extended four times ten.
Would Mary have been so bold to play her part in
   the greatest story ever told,
If perhaps—she had known what her Son would
   endure?
You left Your Word in written form,
Scrolls of parchment now restored,
Stories of Your children's faith
For me to replicate.
If perhaps—
I can blindly trust to see,
Not merely characters surviving like me,
But those who placed themselves in Your hands,
Finding the Promised Land.

From the Outside

You've watched from the outside
What I go through on the inside,
You've changed your life, just for me.
Even though I know you wouldn't have it any other
  way,
Oh, how I wish this wasn't your day by day.
Crying out in confusion and pain,
My heart pains for yours, knowing what you've seen,
Ugly, torn, broken and scary.
I understand how watching has made you weary.
It's lonely walking a road of grief,
Bravely sitting, hoping it's brief.
Only God can see what you see,
He holds your hand while you hold me,
Waiting for healing, relief,
Never more to watch from the outside of me.

One Story

Can I write a story
To say I love you?
It would make you jump for joy,
Or laugh, or dance, perhaps a sigh,
Delighting from characters crafted,
Expertly written for emotion to be extracted.
Just one story, because I miss you
And the words that we've shared,
Together.

About the Author

Carolyn Staffieri is a wife, mother of two, and grandmother who lives in Lancaster, PA.

She found her gift and love for writing poetry during her journey with epilepsy and began using it in earnest over the past two years. Poetry is her expression of God's ever-present faithfulness throughout her life.

Thank you for reading
With Me: A Poetic Expression of God's Faithfulness
Follow Carolyn on social media
for more poetry and book updates
Instagram: @carolynspoetry
Facebook: @carolynspoetry

To purchase additional copies of this book, please visit:
carolynspoetry.com